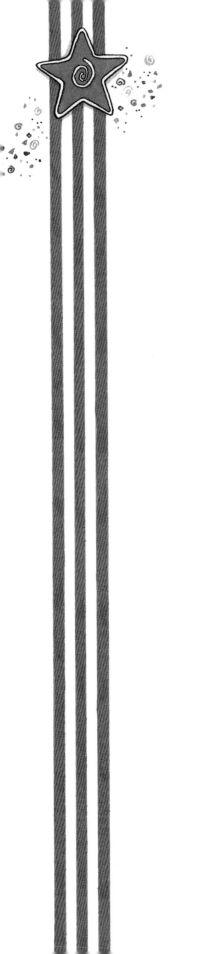

Contents

W9-CAB-191

Star-Spangled Crafts

KATHY ROSS
Illustrated by Sharon Lane Holm

The Millbrook Press
Brookfield, Connecticut

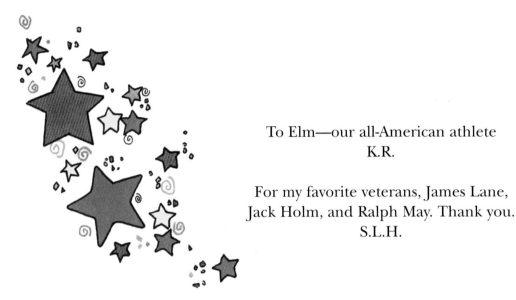

To Elm—our all-American athlete
K.R.

For my favorite veterans, James Lane,
Jack Holm, and Ralph May. Thank you.
S.L.H.

Library of Congress Cataloging-in-Publication Data
Ross, Kathy, (Katharine Reynolds), 1948–
Star-spangled crafts / Kathy Ross ; illustrated by Sharon Lane Holm.
p. cm.
Summary: Provides instructions for creating a variety of crafts with patriotic themes,
including a firecracker lapel pin, flag mosaic, American eagle magnet, fireworks trinket box,
Liberty Bell favors, and more.
ISBN 0-7613-2853-X (lib. bdg.) — ISBN 0-7613-1777-5 (pbk.)
1. Holiday decorations—Juvenile literature. 2. Patriotism in art—Juvenile literature. 3. Fourth of
July—Juvenile literature. 4. Memorial Day—Juvenile literature. [1. Patriotism in art. 2. Holiday
decorations. 3. Handicraft.] I. Holm, Sharon Lane, ill. II. Title.
TT900.H6 R6697 2003   745.5—dc21   2002002400

Published by The Millbrook Press, Inc.
2 Old New Milford Road
Brookfield, Connecticut 06804
www.millbrookpress.com

Printed in the United States of America
5 4 3 2 1 (lib.)
5 4 3 2 1 (pbk.)

You can wear this little firecracker on your collar.

Firecracker Lapel Pin

You need:

discarded red marker cap from a fat marker

two tiny wiggle eyes

tiny pom-pom or bead

white craft glue

pin back

red, gold, and blue sparkle stems

scissors

What you do:

1 Cut six 2 ½-inch (6-cm) pieces of sparkle stem. Curl three of the pieces around your finger.

2 Glue the ends of all six pieces of sparkle stem inside the marker cap to look like the top of an exploding firecracker.

3 Glue the two wiggle eyes and the pom-pom nose to the top part of the outside of the marker cap firecracker.

4 Glue the pin back to the back of the firecracker.

POP!

Here's a new way to display the red, white, and blue.

Ribbon Flag Magnet

You need:

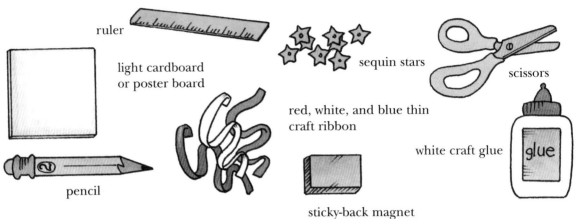

ruler

light cardboard
or poster board

sequin stars

scissors

red, white, and blue thin
craft ribbon

white craft glue   glue

pencil

sticky-back magnet

What you do:

1 Cut seven 4-inch (10-cm) pieces of red ribbon
and six 4-inch pieces of white ribbon.

2 Beginning in the corner of
the piece of cardboard, glue a
piece of red ribbon along the
top edge. Glue a piece of
white ribbon underneath it.
Alternate colors, ending with
a red piece, to make the
stripes of the flag.

3 Trim around the flag to
remove the excess
cardboard and even out the
ends of the ribbons.

 Cut seven 1½-inch (3.8-cm) pieces of the blue ribbon.

 Glue the blue ribbon pieces to the top left corner of the flag, side-by-side, to make the blue field for the stars.

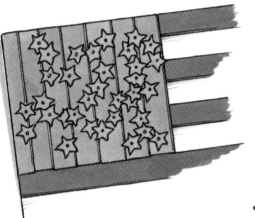

 Cover the blue ribbon field with glue and sprinkle it with gold sequin stars.

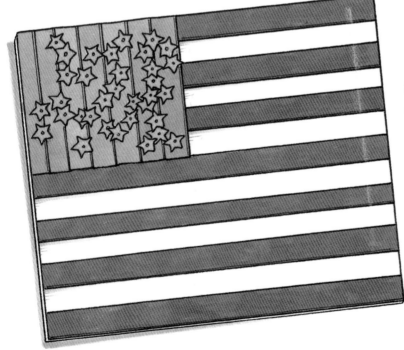 Put a piece of sticky-back magnet on the back of the flag.

Stick your flag magnet on the refrigerator to remind you of the wonderful country you live in.

Legend tells us that Betsy Ross made the first American flag in 1776, and it was adopted by Congress as our flag a year later.

Betsy Ross's Colonial Hat

You need:

scissors

white tissue paper

black thin craft ribbon

What you do:

1 Open a sheet of tissue paper and cut as large a circle as you can from the paper. It should be about 16 inches (40 cm) across.

2 Fold about 2 inches (5 cm) of the circle over. About an inch in from the edge of the circle, cut a 2-inch (5-cm) slit—1-inch (2.5-cm) on the fold, so that it will be 2 inches when unfolded. Measure about an inch, and then cut another slit just like the first. Then measure about 2 inches and cut another slit, then after 1 inch, another slit. What you are doing is cutting pairs of slits, an inch apart from each other, with each grouping about 2 inches apart.

3 Cut a 3-foot (90-cm) length of the black ribbon.

4 Weave the ribbon in and out of the slits all the way around the hat.

5 Carefully pull the ribbon tight until the hat is gathered and exactly fits your head.

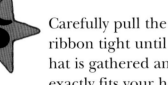

6 Tie the ends of the ribbon in a bow. Trim off any excess ribbon from the ends.

You can make a more long-lasting colonial hat by using white cotton fabric instead of tissue paper.

9

Make this unusual flag to hang in celebration of Flag Day on June 14.

Flag Mosaic

You need:

light cardboard or poster board

red construction paper

red ribbon

scissors

white craft glue

glue

red, white, blue, and yellow disposable plastic containers (laundry detergent container work well)

What you do:

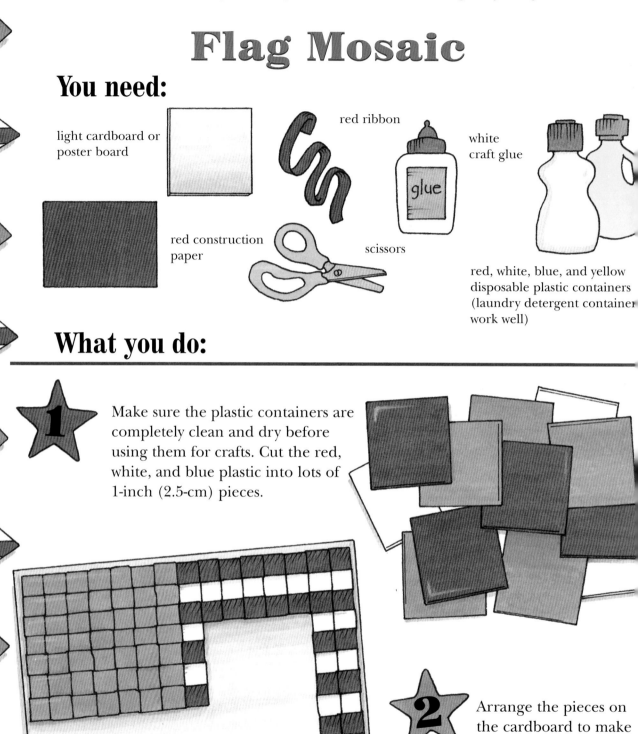

1 Make sure the plastic containers are completely clean and dry before using them for crafts. Cut the red, white, and blue plastic into lots of 1-inch (2.5-cm) pieces.

2 Arrange the pieces on the cardboard to make an American flag.

3 When you are happy with the arrangement of the plastic pieces, glue them to the cardboard.

4 When the glue has dried, trim away the excess cardboard around the flag.

5 Cut stars from the yellow plastic. Glue the stars on the blue section of the flag mosaic.

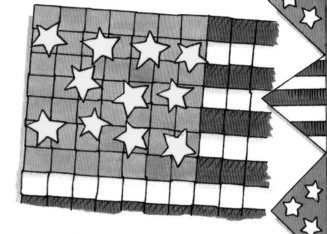

6 Cut a 2-foot (60-cm) piece of the red ribbon. Glue one end of the ribbon near each of the top corners of the back of the cardboard to make a hanger for the flag.

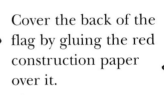

7 Cover the back of the flag by gluing the red construction paper over it.

This flag mosaic would look wonderful hanging on your front door.

Make this patriotic red, white, and blue tassel to top off the antenna of the family car.

Patriotic Antenna Tassel

You need:

1¼-inch (3-cm) Styrofoam ball

red, white, and/or blue map pins

scissors

three sequin stars

red, white, and blue long balloons

What you do:

1 Carefully cut down the center of each balloon, stopping about 2 inches (5 cm) from the blowing end.

2 Slide the uncut end of the blue balloon over the Styrofoam ball.

3 Slide the white balloon over the blue balloon, so that the two cut sides are on either side of the blue balloon.

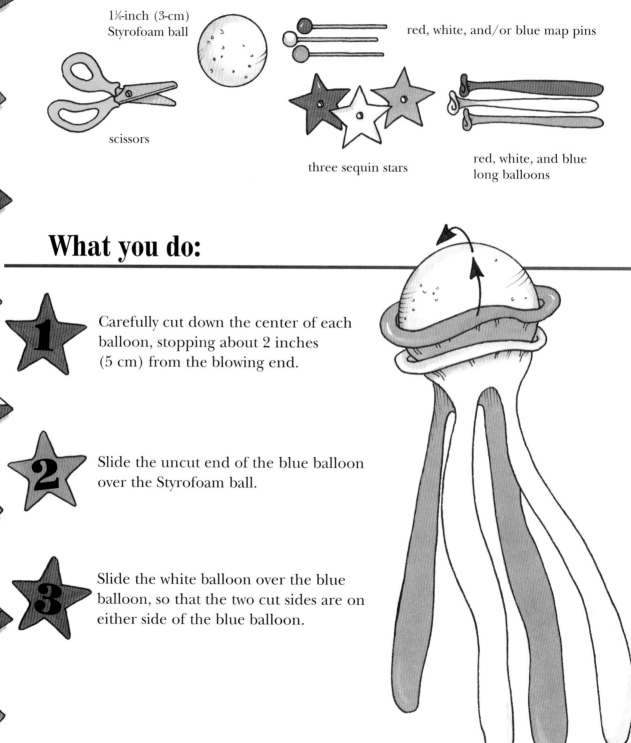

4 Finally, slide the red balloon over the white balloon so that the two sides of the red balloon are on the outside of the white balloon.

5 Carefully cut each strip of balloon in half again, stopping at the Styrofoam ball. This will create the red, white, and blue tassels.

6 Use the map pins to attach sequin stars to the side of the Styrofoam ball.

Slide the ball onto the car antenna through the opening in the mouth of the balloons. If a pin is in the way, just slide it out and re-insert it at an angle so that it does not block the center path for the tip of the antenna.

On Memorial Day, celebrated on the last Monday in May, you will often see veterans selling poppies in memory of those people who died for our country.

Memorial Day Poppy

You need:

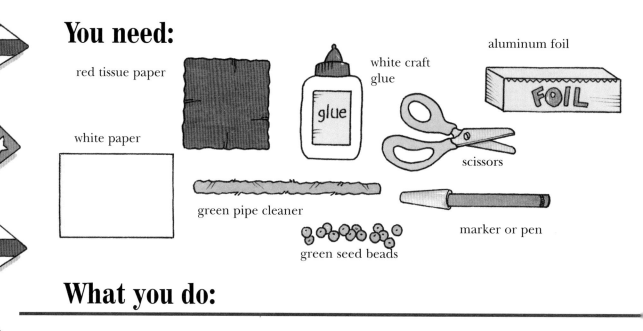

red tissue paper

white paper

white craft glue

aluminum foil

scissors

green pipe cleaner

green seed beads

marker or pen

What you do:

1 Cut a 3-inch (8-cm) square of aluminum foil and a 3-inch square of red tissue paper.

2 Glue the red tissue square over the aluminum foil square. Let the glue dry completely before continuing.

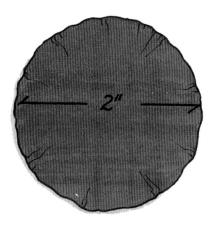

3 Cut a 2-inch (5-cm) circle from the tissue-covered foil to make the poppy.

2"

4 Poke a 6-inch (15-cm) piece of green pipe cleaner through the center of the poppy for the stem. Bend the end of the stem to one side and glue it to the center of the flower.

5 Cover the center of the poppy with glue. Sprinkle the glue with green seed beads to make the center of the poppy.

Memorial Day

6 Cut a thin 4-inch strip (10-cm) from the white paper. Fold the strip of paper in half and glue it around the stem of the poppy.

7 Use the marker or pen to write Memorial Day and the date on the paper strip.

You can stick the stem of the poppy through a buttonhole to wear it on Memorial Day.

Memorial Day

The proud bald eagle is the national bird of the United States of America.

American Eagle Magnet

You need:

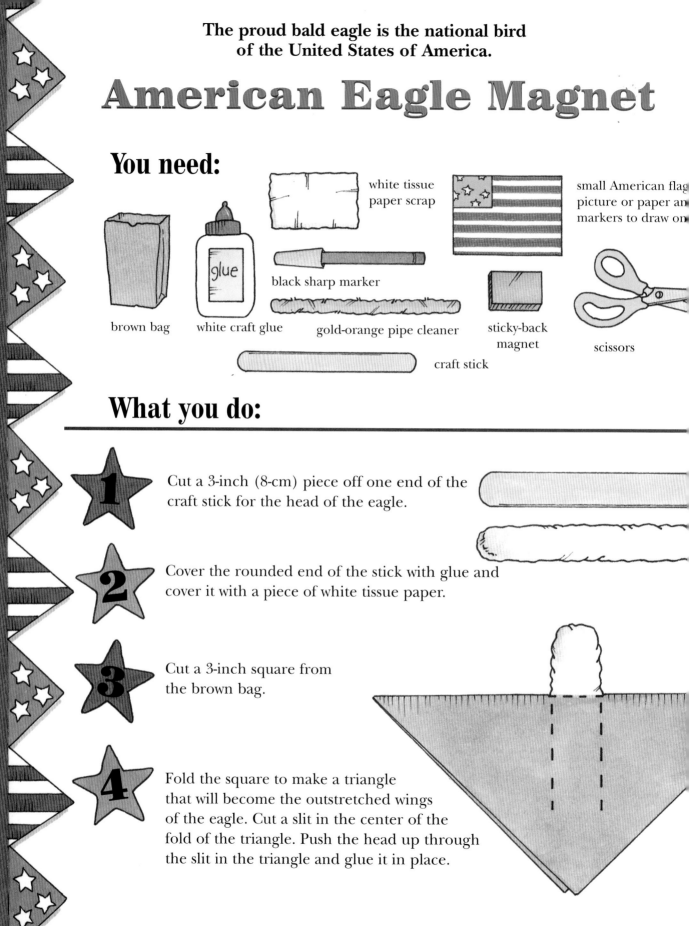

white tissue paper scrap

small American flag picture or paper an markers to draw on

black sharp marker

brown bag

white craft glue

gold-orange pipe cleaner

sticky-back magnet

scissors

craft stick

What you do:

1 Cut a 3-inch (8-cm) piece off one end of the craft stick for the head of the eagle.

2 Cover the rounded end of the stick with glue and cover it with a piece of white tissue paper.

3 Cut a 3-inch square from the brown bag.

4 Fold the square to make a triangle that will become the outstretched wings of the eagle. Cut a slit in the center of the fold of the triangle. Push the head up through the slit in the triangle and glue it in place.

Cut a tail for the eagle from the brown bag. Cover the tail with a piece of white tissue paper. Glue the top of the tail between the front and back of the triangle wings to hang down in the center of the eagle.

 Fold a tiny piece of pipe cleaner in half for the beak. Glue the beak on one side of the head so that it looks as if the head of the eagle is turned sideways. Use the black marker to give the eagle an eye.

 Draw or cut out a picture of the American flag to glue behind the eagle.

 Put a piece of sticky-back magnet on the back of the eagle.

Gracie

dog
cat

Stick this proud bird on your refrigerator to hold school papers that you are proud of.

Patriotic Puppet Pals

You need:

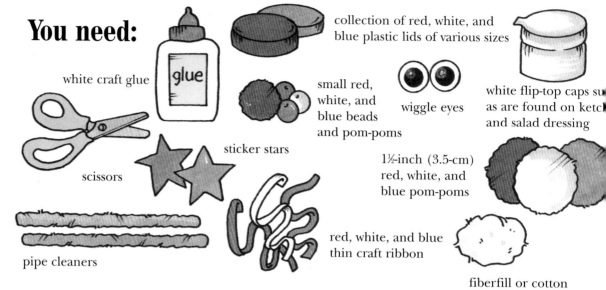

white craft glue

scissors

sticker stars

collection of red, white, and blue plastic lids of various sizes

small red, white, and blue beads and pom-poms

wiggle eyes

white flip-top caps su as are found on ketc and salad dressing

1½-inch (3.5-cm) red, white, and blue pom-poms

red, white, and blue thin craft ribbon

pipe cleaners

fiberfill or cotton

What you do:

1 Select a flip-top cap for the head of the puppet. Turn the cap upside down so that the top becomes the bottom jaw of the head and the opening becomes the mouth.

2 Glue on a pom-pom for hair.

3 Glue on wiggle eyes and a pom-pom or bead nose for the face.

Turn a plastic lid on the edge for the body of the puppet.

Select a smaller lid for the base to support the body. Fill the small lid with glue, then cotton or fiberfill. Cover the cotton with glue and glue the edge of the body lid to the cotton-filled base lid.

Glue the head to the top of the body lid. Let the puppet dry, undisturbed, before continuing.

Decorate the puppet with ribbon bows and sticker stars. You might want to make a bead necklace for one puppet, using the pipe cleaner and some craft beads.

Open and close the head lid of the puppet to make it "talk."

Fireworks are often a part of celebrating Independence Day.

Fireworks Trinket Box

You need:

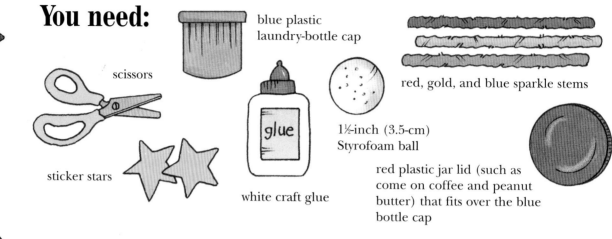

scissors

blue plastic laundry-bottle cap

red, gold, and blue sparkle stems

sticker stars

glue

white craft glue

1½-inch (3.5-cm) Styrofoam ball

red plastic jar lid (such as come on coffee and peanut butter) that fits over the blue bottle cap

What you do:

1 The blue cap will be the bottom of the container and the red lid the top. Make sure that both lids have been washed thoroughly.

2 Cut the Styrofoam ball in half. Glue the flat side of one half of the ball to the top center of the red lid. (Save the other half for another project.)

3 Cut several 6-inch (15-cm) pieces of sparkle stem. Wrap each stem around your finger to make a spiral.

4 Dip the end of each spiral in glue, then poke it into the Styrofoam ball on top of the red lid.

5 Cover the Styrofoam half with sparkle stems to look like exploding fireworks.

6 Decorate the blue lid with sticker stars.

Keep coins or other small items in this container.

Popping Firecracker Puppet

You need:

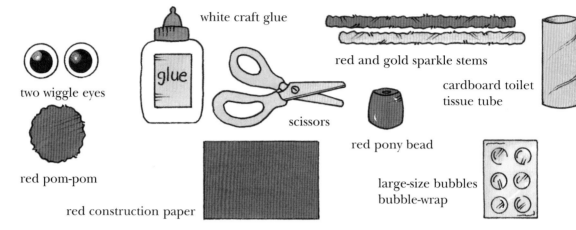

two wiggle eyes

white craft glue

glue

red pom-pom

scissors

red construction paper

red and gold sparkle stems

cardboard toilet tissue tube

red pony bead

large-size bubbles
bubble-wrap

What you do:

1 Cut a piece of construction paper to exactly fit around the cardboard tube to cover it. Glue the red paper in place around the tube. This will be the firecracker.

2 Wrap six 6-inch (15-cm) pieces of the sparkle stems around your finger to curl them.

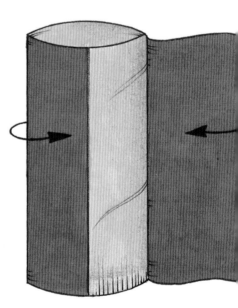

 Glue the ends of the stems inside the top of the firecracker so that it looks like it is exploding.

 Glue a face on the top front of the firecracker so that the sparkle stems come out from the back top of the tube, behind the face. Glue on two wiggle eyes, a pom-pom nose and the pony bead for a mouth.

Cut a row of seven unpopped bubbles from the bubble wrap. Slide the bubbles inside the bottom part of the firecracker.

To use the firecracker puppet, slide your finger in through the bottom of the puppet and squeeze the bubbles to make a popping sound. Have extra bubble wrap on hand to "reload."

POP!

POP!

Make your own patriotic flying disc to play with at a Fourth of July picnic.

Patriotic Flying Disc

You need:

two 9-inch (23-cm)
red plastic plates

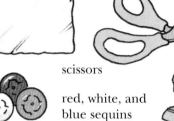

gallon-size clear
plastic bag

scissors

red, white, and
blue sequins

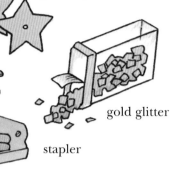

gold sequin stars

gold glitter

stapler

What you do:

1 Cut the center out of both red plastic plates without cutting through the edge. (Hint: save the plate centers to make the heart necklace found on page 42–43.)

2 Put a small amount of the sequins and glitter into the plastic bag.

24

3 Place the filled bag over the top of one of the plate rims.

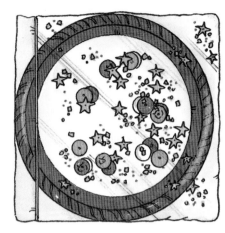

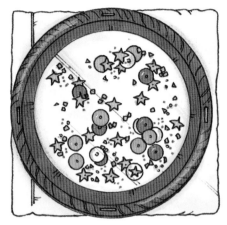

4 Cover the first rim and the bag with the second rim, making sure the contents of the bag are all in the center portion of the rims.

5 Pull the edges of the bag tight across the bottom rim and staple the two rims together. Make sure the plastic is pulled tight across the rim.

6 Trim the excess plastic bag from around the outside of the rims. Shake the flying disc to evenly distribute the sequins and glitter in the center.

Dogs love flying discs, but better to toss this one with a human friend!

Patriotic Headband

You need:

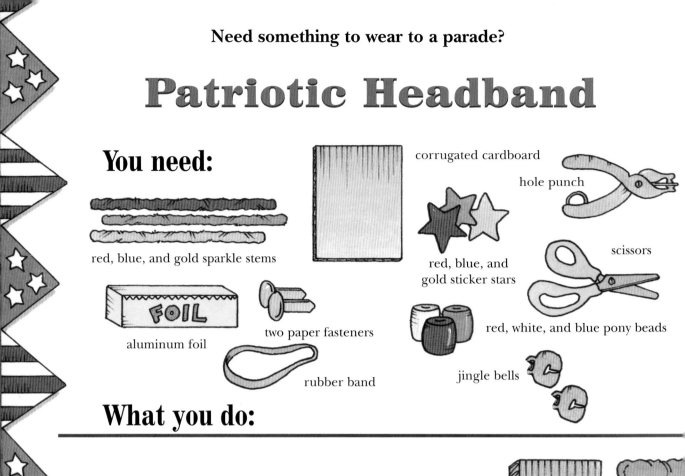

red, blue, and gold sparkle stems

aluminum foil

two paper fasteners

rubber band

corrugated cardboard

red, blue, and gold sticker stars

hole punch

scissors

red, white, and blue pony beads

jingle bells

What you do:

1 Cut a strip of corrugated cardboard 1½ by 12 inches (3.5 x 30 cm). Make sure that the holes in the cardboard are open on the long end of the strip so that you will be able to insert the ends of the sparkle stems through them.

2 Wrap the cardboard with aluminum foil.

3 Wrap the three sparkle stems around your finger to make them spiral.

4 Slide some pony beads and a jingle bell on the sparkle stems.

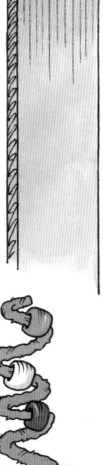

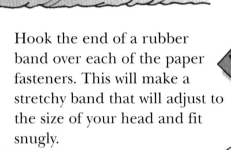

Poke the end of each stem through the foil on a long end of the corrugated strip and into the holes in the cardboard to secure them. Decorate the front of the strip with some sticker stars.

Punch a hole in each end of the strip.

Insert a paper fastener into each hole and bend the ends out to secure.

Hook the end of a rubber band over each of the paper fasteners. This will make a stretchy band that will adjust to the size of your head and fit snugly.

Put on your patriotic headband and go cheer the marching bands.

The Statue of Liberty stands in New York Harbor, a symbol of hope for many people coming to our country.

Statue of Liberty Crown

You need:

scissors

a paintbrush

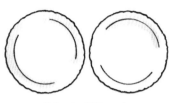

two 9-inch (30-cm)
uncoated white paper plates

gold paint

newspaper to
work on

stapler

What you do:

1 Cut across the center part of one plate without cutting through the rim.

2 Cut across the plate the other way so you have four equal wedge shapes.

3 Cut each wedge shape in half so you have eight wedge-shaped points.

4 Cut through the rim and remove one pie-shaped section, including the rim.

Cut the center out of the second plate without cutting the rim.

6 Fold out all the points of the first plate.

7 Set the folded points on the rim of the second plate and staple them to that rim, spreading the band of points so that they go about three-quarters of the way around the circle. This will be the Liberty crown.

8 Paint the crown gold on both sides. It is best to paint one side and let it dry before painting the second side.

Wear your Liberty crown to a patriotic party or parade.

Hang this wreath on your front door on Election Day to remind people to vote.

Pinwheel Wreath

You need:

white craft glue

red, white, and blue construction paper

gold sticker stars

scissors

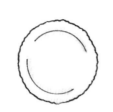
9-inch (30-cm) uncoated white paper plate

large paper clip

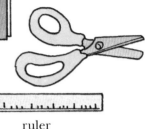
ruler

What you do:

1 Cut three 4-inch (10-cm) squares from each of the three colors of construction paper.

2 Fold each of the nine squares in half to make triangles.

3 Cut the center from the paper plate without cutting the rim. The rim will be the base for the wreath.

4 Arrange the nine triangles around the rim of the wreath as shown, alternating the three colors.

When you are happy with your arrangement, glue the triangles to the plate rim and to each other where they overlap.

 Decorate the wreath with sticker stars.

 Slide the large paper clip over the top of the plate frame so that the end sticks up to use as a hanger.

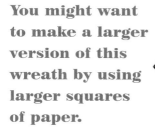

You might want to make a larger version of this wreath by using larger squares of paper.

Presidents' Day, celebrated in February, is a day to honor our great presidents.

George Washington and Abraham Lincoln Puppets

You need:

- scissors
- white craft glue
- a paintbrush
- black yarn
- large paper clips
- map pin
- newspaper
- black and blue poster paint
- black and red markers
- masking tape
- white and blue construction-paper scraps
- small yogurt container with edge (such as are found when you purchase six containers attached together)
- thin black ribbon
- cotton or fiberfill
- white facial tissue

What you do to make the basic puppet:

1 Close a double sheet of newspaper. Fold it in half from top to bottom.

2 Starting on the edge that is not folded, roll the newspaper into a tube to make the body of the puppet.

3 Secure the fold with glue.

4 Slide a paper clip over each end of the tube to hold the rolled newspaper in place until the glue dries.

5 Paint the entire newspaper tube blue to make a George Washington puppet and black to make an Abraham Lincoln puppet. For Lincoln, you will also need to paint the outside of the yogurt container black for a top hat.

To make George Washington:

Wrap four inches (10 cm) at one end of the tube with masking tape to make the head.

Use the markers to draw a face on the masking tape.

Glue cotton around the face and on the back of the head for hair. Tie the back of the cotton hair with a black ribbon to resemble the style of colonial times.

Wrap a piece of folded tissue around the neck of the puppet for a collar. Secure the collar with glue. Stick a map pin in the center of the tissue collar to look like a stickpin.

Cut a blue paper rectangle to wrap around the puppet for a coat. Fold the top corners back in the front of the paper coat to look like lapels.

To make Abe Lincoln:

★ Wrap four inches (10 cm) at one end of the tube with masking tape to make the head.

★ Use the markers to draw a face on the masking tape.

★ Glue the yogurt container to the top of the puppet for the top hat. Glue the band of black ribbon around the hat to make the hatband.

★ Cut a triangle from the white paper to look like a shirtfront under a black suit. Add details to the shirt with the black marker.

★ Glue yarn bits around the face for a beard and over the sides and back of the head for hair.

You might want to make puppets of other presidents to add to your puppet collection.

Uncle Sam is a symbolic patriotic figure with the initials, U.S.

Uncle Sam Lapel Pin

You need:

white craft glue

gold sequin stars

scissors

glue

pin back

markers

toothpick

fiberfill

wooden ice cream spoon

two red sequins

What you do:

1 Cut the pointed ends off the toothpick. Use a marker to color the toothpick blue.

2 Color the handle end of the spoon red and blue for the hat. Color the eating end of the spoon pink for the face.

3 Draw eyes, nose and a mouth on the face with markers.

4 Glue the toothpick across the bottom. Glue fiberfill around the face for hair and a beard.

5 Glue the two sequins on each side of the mouth for cheeks. Decorate the hatband by gluing on some star sequins.

6 Glue a pin back to the back of the spoon.

You can also use this project as a magnet by attaching a piece of sticky-back magnet to the back in place of the pin back.

The Liberty Bell rang in 1776 to announce the signing of the Declaration of Independence.

Liberty Bell Favor

You need:

gold sticker stars

corrugated cardboard

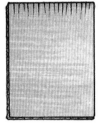

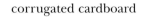

gold sparkle stem

small round lollipop

FOIL

aluminum foil

pen

What you do:

1 Cut a 4- to 5-inch (10- to 13-cm) bell shape from the corrugated cardboard. Be sure you cut the bell so that the holes in between the front and back layer of the cardboard are at the top and the bottom of the bell.

2 Cut a 3-inch (8-cm) piece of the sparkle stem.

3 Slide the two ends of the sparkle stem into the top of the bell to make a ring shaped holder for the bell.

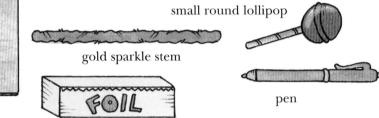

Unwrap the lollipop. Rewrap the lollipop with aluminum foil.

 Slide the stick of the lollipop up through the hole at the center of the bottom of the bell so that the lollipop forms the clapper of the bell.

6 Decorate the bell with a line of sticker stars. You might want to put on just enough stars to write out the letters of the name of the person the favor is for. Use the pen to write a letter on each star.

If you don't want to use a candy, slide a jingle bell on a small piece of sparkle stem and attach it to the bottom of the bell in place of the lollipop.

In 1961, Congress passed a resolution that officially recognized Samuel Wilson of Troy, New York, as the person who first inspired the symbol of Uncle Sam.

Newspaper Uncle Sam

You need:

a paintbrush

large paper clips

scissors

pink and blue poster paint

newspaper

white craft glue

hole punch

cotton or fiberfill

red and blue construct paper scraps

sticker stars

red and white thin craft ribbon

small flag picture or white paper and markers to draw a flag

red pipe cleaner

What you do:

1 Fold a single sheet of newspaper in half, side-to-side.

2 Starting at the edge opposite the fold, roll the newspaper and secure the roll with glue. Secure the roll until the glue dries by sliding paper clips over each end of the newspaper tube.

3 Repeat these steps with a second sheet of newspaper.

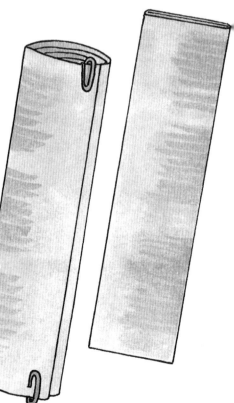

4 Flatten out the two rolled tubes. Glue them together in an X shape to form two up-raised arms and two spread legs.

5 Fold and roll a third sheet of newspaper, but do not glue it. Allow the ends to spread so that, when you flatten them, they are about 3½-inches (9 cm) across.

3½"

6 Fold the third tube in half and glue the ends over the front and back of the X shape, so that it forms the body, head, and hat for Uncle Sam.

7 Paint the ends of the arms pink for hands and a 2-inch (5-cm) section above the arms pink for the face. Paint the rest of the newspaper figure blue.

8 Use the hole punch to punch out eyes from blue paper and a mouth from the red paper. Glue them in place on the face.

9 Cut a band from the red paper to make a brim for the hat. Glue the band across the top of the pink face.

10 Glue on a cotton or fiberfill beard and some hair.

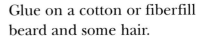

Decorate the blue costume and hat with bands of red and white ribbon and sticker stars.

 Draw an American flag or use a picture of one cut from a magazine or printed off the Internet.

13 Glue the flag to one end of a 6-inch (15-cm) piece of the red pipe cleaner. Glue the other end of the pipe cleaner to the hand of the figure to look like he is holding it.

Cut a 2-foot (60-cm) length of ribbon. Thread the ribbon through the fold at the top of the hat. Tie the two ends of the ribbon together to make a hanger for the figure.

This Uncle Sam looks wonderful hanging on a sheltered front door or in a window.

Make these coasters to use at your Independence Day celebration.

Patriotic Party Coasters

You need:

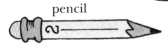

four discarded
compact discs (CDs)

pencil

clear cellophane tape

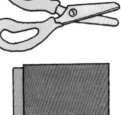

scissors

glue

white craft glue

small patriotic pictures
printed from the Internet or cut
from old magazines and catalogs

red and blue construction paper

What you do:

1 Use the pencil to trace around each CD on the construction paper. Cut the circles out.

2 Glue a small patriotic picture to the center of each circle so that it can be seen through the clear center portion of a CD.

3 Cover each picture with cellophane tape to protect it from moisture.

4 Glue a circle to the printed side of each CD so that the picture can be seen in the center of the silver side.

If you are expecting lots of guests to join your celebration you might want to make more than four coasters.

This flag folk-art necklace is fun and easy to make.

Heart Flag Necklace

You need:

scissors

white craft glue

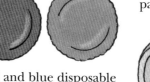

glue

red and blue disposable plastic plates

gold sequin stars

paper clip

white thin craft ribbon

masking tape

What you do:

1 Cut a 3-inch (8-cm) heart from the red plastic plate.

2 Cut a piece from the blue plastic plate to cover the top left section of the red heart.

3 Glue three strips of white ribbon across the heart. Trim off the excess ribbon on each end of the strips.

4 Glue the blue piece over the top left bump of the heart.

Cover the blue piece with glue and sprinkle with the gold sequin stars.

Glue the paper clip to the top center of the back of the heart so that half of the clip sticks up to form a hanger for the heart necklace. Cover the glued paper clip with a piece of masking tape to hold it in position while it dries.

Cut a 3-foot (60-cm) length of ribbon. Thread the ribbon through the paper clip and tie the ends together to make a necklace.

Hooray for the U.S.A.!

43

Give a tissue box a patriotic look with this project.

Uncle Sam Tissue Box

You need:

 scissors

white craft glue

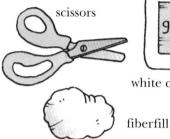 fiberfill

1-inch red pom-pom

two large wiggle eyes

sticker stars

 red and blue construction paper

 square box of white tissues

What you do:

1 Turn the tissue box on one side so that the top tissue hangs down to form a white beard for Uncle Sam.

2 Glue the two wiggle eyes above the beard, on the clear plastic over the opening of the box.

3 Glue the red pom-pom below the eyes for a nose.

 Cut a 4-inch square from the blue paper for the hat.

 Cut stripes for the hat from the red paper and glue them in place.

 Cut a strip of red paper for the brim of the hat. Glue the brim across the bottom of the hat.

 Decorate the hat with sticker stars.

 Glue the hat to the tissue box above the eyes. Glue fiberfill on each side of the head for hair.

This is a usable tissue dispenser. When one tissue "beard" is pulled out, another one will appear.

Celebrate the red, white, and blue with this name pin.

Red, White, and Blue Name Pin

You need:

scissors

white craft glue

glue

pin back

ruler

blue and red
fat markers

plastic lid for drying

tiny gold star sequins

macaroni letters or
craft bead letters

white string

newspaper
to work on

NEWS

What you do:

1 Cut three 5-inch (13-cm) pieces of string.

2 Working on newspaper, use the fat markers to color one string red and another string blue. Leave the third string white.

3 Cut the three strings in half. Put a band of glue across the plastic lid.

4 Set the six strings in the glue, one above the other, alternating the three colors, to make a red, white, and blue band. Do not worry about uneven edges. You will trim them later.

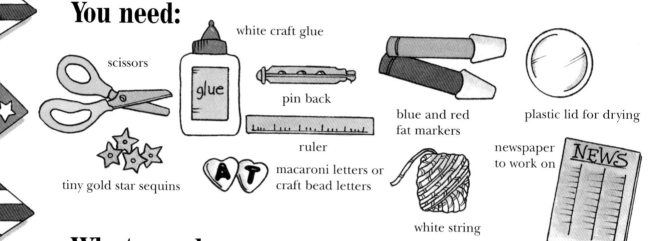

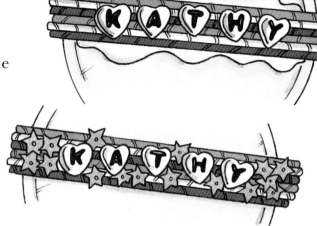

5. Find the letters to spell your name. Cover the top of the string band with glue and arrange the letters across the band. Do not rub the glue around too much or you will smear the colors.

6. Sprinkle star sequins in the glue around the letters. Cover the sequins and letters with more glue. Do not worry about covering the letters. When the glue is dry it will be clear. Let the pin dry completely overnight.

7. Peel the pin off the lid. Use the scissors to trim the edges of the string band so they are even on both sides of the pin.

8. Glue a pin back to the back of the pin.

Name pins make great favors for a patriotic party or picnic.

About the Author and Artist

Thirty years as a teacher and director of nursery school programs has given Kathy Ross extensive experience in guiding young children through craft projects. Among the more than forty craft books she has written are *Crafts for All Seasons, Make Yourself a Monster, Crafts From Your Favorite Children's Songs, Kathy Ross Crafts Letter Shapes,* and *Play-Doh™ Fun and Games.* To find out more about Kathy, visit her Web site: *www.Kathyross.com.*

Sharon Lane Holm, a resident of Fairfield, Connecticut, won awards for her work in advertising design before shifting her concentration to children's books. Her recent books include *Sidewalk Games Around the World, Happy Birthday, Everywhere!, Happy New Year, Everywhere!,* and *Merry Christmas, Everywhere!,* all by Arlene Erlbach; and *Beautiful Bats* by Linda Glaser.

Together, Kathy Ross and Sharon Lane Holm have also created *The Best Christmas Crafts Ever!,* as well as the popular Holiday Crafts for Kids series and the Crafts for Kids Who Are Wild About series.